MW00963391

SHADOWS ON THE WALL

Life Is What You Make IT

D. RICHARD DEAN

ISBN 10: 1494291517
ISBN 13: 9781494291518

Definition of a shadow: "a hint or faint image or idea; intimation: shadows of things to come"

INTRODUCTION

A LONG TIME ago in a land far away, a golf tournament began. I played with three of my four sons. The tournament, held on a course near Philadelphia, was sponsored by a company associated with one of my sons. My boys are all good golfers. I am not! There were probably ten foursomes—all sponsored by local businesses. Almost all of these men were very good golfers. Most played three or four times a week. Their skill levels were very high. They weren't professionals, but they were close to it.

I didn't really want to play because, as I said, I am not very good, and I don't play very often. But my boys persuaded me to give it a try. I saw this as a day with my boys, whom I don't see very often. They live in different states far apart from each other and far from me.

Well, play began. We were the fourth or fifth foursome to tee off. It was a beautiful day, about seventy five degrees. The greens glistened. A slight breeze moved the trees. The fairways were elegant. I played my usual game. Some good holes, some bad ones. And some that were terrible. About the fourth or fifth hole, we received a visit from the tournament marshal.

"You boys will have to speed up your game," the marshal said. "You're too slow and you're holding up the other teams."

One of the reasons I am not a very good player is that I get very nervous when I feel I am holding up someone else, or when someone is holding me up. My patience is limited. When the marshal told us to speed up, I felt like quitting right there. Had it not been for my boys, I probably would have. So we continued and tried to speed up, although not very successfully.

In any case, we managed to finish the tournament and our scores were very predictable. At the conclusion, my sons voted me the one to cart our clubs back to the car. I complied.

When I came back to the course, I saw my sons standing by an enormous scoreboard. I drove up and said to my oldest son, who was really the best golfer in our group, "What are you guys looking at?" At which point, in unison, they said, "Dad, you're tied for the lead in this tournament!" I said, "That's impossible!"

But as I looked at the scoreboard, I saw that it was true. I was tied for the lead. How could this be possible?

It was then I learned the tournament was being conducted under Callaway rules. You may wonder, what does that mean? That's the same question I asked. How is this possible? Then I learned that under Callaway rules, the erratic golfer has a real chance. Someone who has ten strokes on one hole but has three strokes on another can compete. Since I was so erratic, I was tied for the lead.

My boys and I were flabbergasted. We couldn't believe what we were seeing, yet it was true.

When the end of the day came and the tournament was concluded, **I won the tournament!** In my wildest dreams, I never thought that would be possible. And from the look on my sons' faces, they never thought it would be possible either. The trophy and plaque still hang on my wall to this day—and the day I won them is one of the proudest in my life.

It just goes to show that you never know. Anything is possible, even what seems like an utter impossibility. The message is, don't give up, and keep trying. Whether you are playing sports, searching for a job, overcoming a health problem or a family issue, or you just want to get your first book published, anything is possible as long as you don't give up.

This text is structured as a series of stories and adventures—all demonstrating the possibilities that lie before us. Many of the stories and examples I have included have been used with my business students in the five different colleges in which I have been an adjunct professor. Whether you are rich or poor, old or young, black or white, Asian or European, single or married, the future is what you make of it! And you can be successful! Anyone can, as long as you continue the journey on this long and winding road. It can last a lifetime and be very exciting.

The collage I am introducing you to is like shadows on a wall. As the day moves on and as the shapes are exposed to sunlight, they change—just as we must change and grow as well. Each shadow tells its own story and each has a lesson.

1

IN THE BEGINNING

I HAD JUST finished teaching my 8 a.m. class in business communication in Villa Marie College in Buffalo, New York, and was packing up my instruction materials when one of my students approached and asked if she could make an appointment to see me in my office. She was working on a project and she thought I might be able to provide her some advice and help.

"How about around eleven today? Because I will have a couple of free hours at that time," I said.

"That will be perfect!" she said. "I'll see you at eleven." And she dashed away to her next class.

Well, she was true to her word and arrived promptly at 11:00 a.m... After some brief small talk, she explained her needs. She was working on developing a paper for her English class regarding teachers she had encountered in the past. In the paper, she wanted to write about a teacher who had the most influence in helping her decide on a career in business. She said, "Professor Dean, you have been my instructor for four different subjects. Your stories about your experience in business have made all the basic business principles easy to understand. What amazes me is that you have never told the same story twice—that you have illustrated each principle, whether it's accounting, marketing, sales, human resources, or manufacturing. How do you do it? No one ever falls asleep in your class. You've got to be one of the world's best storytellers." I said, "Sheila, why don't I give you a picture of my career through the various stages it has gone then you can pick and choose just what you want to use. It might be a little long, but I am sure you will find it quite interesting. Let me start at the beginning."

The year was 1938. The Nazi war machine was just beginning its rape of Europe. In a small town in western New York, I was born. My father was a milkman—a person who delivered milk via horse and wagon. And my mother was a schoolteacher coming from a one-room school house. Life was simple for me in those years. There was no TV, or the Internet, or computers, but only the radio.

My grandfather (Hugh McVeigh) was an Irish farmer who really loved baseball, in particular the New York Yankees. He would follow them on the radio each day. Each Yankee game, whether played at home or away, they'd broadcast live. My parents, my sister, and I lived on my grandfather's farm for much of my early years. When we first moved in, there was no indoor plumbing (we had outside toilets), no running water (there was an outside pump), and no internal heating system other than an enormous kitchen stove that provided the heat source for the whole house. However, shortly after we arrived, my parents had a plumbing system with toilets and running water installed. They also had a coal furnace installed. Heaven had arrived.

Life was pleasant on the farm, which stood on the banks of the Erie Canal. One time, I asked my mother if it was difficult on the farm during the Great Depression of 1929, when the whole United States was struggling. She said she never knew there was a depression because on a farm they grew their own food—vegetables—and they had their own animals. And they prospered because they sold or traded the extra to those people who were having a much more difficult time.

I grew up, went to grade school and then high school, and in 1954 went to work part-time for a local veterinarian. When I graduated from high school in 1956, I automatically went to work for the vet on a full-time basis. No thought was ever given to college. In those days, most high school graduates simply went to work after graduation. I did the same. That is, until something changed my mind and my life.

2

GOING TO COLLEGE

TO BE SUCCESSFUL in college is really not as difficult as it first seems. It's simply a matter of following a game plan and sticking to it even when it gets tough. Just remember hundreds of thousands of people have done it. You can too.

I was not a very good high school student. I didn't like high school. I didn't see any value to education. It seemed to be a waste of time dealing with subject matter that no one would use anyway. To me, it was like taking medicine. Let me swallow it quickly and get it over with. I was a C student—just putting in my time until I finished. During my junior year, I obtained a part-time job with a local veterinary hospital cleaning kennels. I liked working with the animals and eventually worked my way up to assistant of animal surgery. I eventually became very good at it and enjoyed the work. The veterinarian came to depend on my skills and my abilities.

When I graduated from high school, the doctor offered me a full-time job. I took it. My skills continued to improve. I was becoming a fast learner and enjoying it. Finally, after about a year, I began to feel like, perhaps, I should become a veterinarian. I discussed it with my boss and he agreed to help. He explained to me that first you had to obtain a four-year degree from the agricultural college and could then apply to veterinary school, which would be another two or three years.

I thought long and hard about this and finally decided that I was going to do it. I went back to my high school guidance counselor and asked for his help. He said, "It's going to be a long, tough road, particularly with your low grades," but he agreed to help. We filled out applications for Cornell, Penn State, Ohio State, and Michigan State Universities. My world collapsed when I was rejected by each of these schools due to my low high school grades. They said I wasn't college material. My attitude, however, had begun to change, and like so many other people, I felt I wanted more. My whole life was ahead of me and I was becoming convinced I wanted something more than just being a veterinarian's kennel assistant.

My guidance counselor and I sat down again to discuss my situation. My college prospects appeared very grim, but he had an idea. He had a friend who was a college professor at Saint Vincent College, a small, Benedictine monastery in Latrobe, Pennsylvania. He talked to his friend and decided I should apply at this school. If, during my first year, my grades were sufficiently high, I could then transfer to one of my primary schools for the second year. It seemed like a good plan. I applied and was accepted. Everything seemed to be coming up roses. My world was about to change.

Well, life isn't always as simple as it seems on the surface. College was much more difficult than I expected. I thought it was just going to be an extension of high school—not so. One of the first lessons I learned was that to become a veterinarian you had to have solid grades in math, chemistry, and the physical sciences. My strengths in high school and now in college were the social sciences: English, History, Sociology, etc. This was a difficult learning experience for me. I had a very difficult fall semester.

During my spring semester at Saint Vincent College, I was faced with a major decision—either give up my dream of becoming a doctor or change to majoring in the social sciences. I chose the latter and decided to pursue a different career. (As of yet, I didn't know what that career would be.)

At the conclusion of my first year, I decided to transfer to a college closer to home, Canisius College in Buffalo. But being closer to home meant many new distractions, which really didn't work in my favor. My grades began to spiral downward. By the conclusion of my second year, I received notification from the college's administrative offices that my grades were too low to continue in education at this college. I was tossed out!

Well, where do I go from here? I decided that with two years of college in my portfolio, there would be many opportunities available. My two years would put me ahead of those who had no college at all. But I was about to learn another major lesson in life. Just having two years of college and no degree meant "no interest." During job interviews, the first question usually asked was, "Why did you drop out of college? Not enough initiative? Hello! We're not really interested. Sorry!"

I went back to working for the same veterinarian for minimum wage. However, my attitude was changing. I wanted something more—just what that more was I didn't know, but I did know that it wouldn't happen without that piece of paper. I made an appointment with the president of Canisius College to plead my case. He listened very patiently to my supplications and my belief that I had learned my lesson.

"Please, just give me another chance. I am ready to do better." He thought long and hard about my request and then he said, "No!" He didn't believe I was college material and thought I should just get on with the rest of my life. I left his office totally devastated. What do I do now? I decided to move on. I bought a used motorcycle and taught myself how to ride. Well, it was about a month later when I had a chance to go to a grand prix of motorcycle racing in Watkins Glen, New York, with a group called the Road Vultures.

This weekend would change my life forever. When I experienced the lifestyle of this raucous group, I made a life-changing decision. I didn't know how I would do it, but I was going back to college and obtaining a degree. I put the motorcycle up for sale and sold it to the first person who looked at it (who, incidentally, was killed on it the first or second time he rode it).

My strategy for college had to change. I called the secretary of the president of Canisius and had a real "heart-to-heart" discussion with her.

She agreed to help me obtain another appointment with her boss. When the time approached for my meeting with the president, I had my hair cut short. I bought a new suit. I dressed for the occasion as if it were a business meeting. My approach was totally different. I simply begged for a second chance. I would do anything he asked. I only wanted a chance to prove that I could do it.

After what seemed like hours, he finally spoke. "Well, we'll see how serious you are. This next semester, you can take one class. If you get an A or B the next semester, we'll follow the same procedure. Again if it's an A or B, we will consider letting you take two or three classes. We will proceed from there one step at a time."

That next semester, I made some major changes in the way I approached education. As a result, I received a B. The following semester, I received an A. I was eventually allowed to return on a part-time basis and was successful, so much so that during my final semester of my senior year I carried a double load of courses and for the first time in my life I made the dean's list. This designation is reserved for those students who are deemed academically superior.

Graduation day was the proudest day of my life. I did it! I received my bachelor's degree in social sciences. Some years later, I did return to college and obtain a master's degree in business as well. I went on to a lengthy career in business, eventually becoming a vice president, a position I initially told you all about. All this took place well before I became a professor in a college business department Well, why did I tell you this story? Because there are some major lessons that I learned that can be valuable to anyone who hopes to obtain a college degree.

I like to tell my students obtaining a college degree is like navigating a fast-moving river. Your goal is to get from one side of the river to the other. Throughout your two years, four years, or six years, there will be many obstacles. There will be problems you must overcome—be it family, finances, or something else. The river has many obstacles. Also, each professor is an individual and looks at a student differently. Professors may put many impediments in the way. Some educators are easy to work with while others can be very difficult. Your success depends on your ability to successfully navigate this stream filled with obstacles—to work within the system that doesn't always seem fair.

But don't give up, even though it will seem difficult at times. Remember, millions before you have arrived successfully on the other shore and obtained the degree they desperately desired. In my case, this success then opened the door for achieving a successful career and can do the same for you. The future is in your hands. Don't be afraid to grab it. It can be very exciting.

3

CAREER DECISIONS

WHEN I FINALLY graduated from college in 1964, the next question was, "What do I do now? Where do I go from here?" Well, since my mother had been a schoolteacher, maybe this was the direction for me. But there was a problem to start with. I had no practical teaching experience, and no teaching certification. Also, I had never spoken in front of a group in my life.

I had heard that the city of Buffalo was in need of English and history teachers in their inner city (no one wanted to get involved as a teacher in the inner-city environment in those days). I applied and was accepted on a provisional basis (since I wasn't yet certified). My starting salary for the school years 1964 and 1965 was $5,000, not really enough even that long ago to raise a family of eventually five children. But luck smiled on me when the veterinarian with whom I used to work said I could work there on a part-time basis to earn a little extra income. However, to maintain my provisional certification, I also had to begin work on a master's degree as well.

My first year as a teacher was very enlightening. I still remember all the students in school 37 in Buffalo assembled in the auditorium on the opening day of school. The principal would read off each student's name and at the appropriate time those students were to follow their home-room teachers to the homeroom. My students' names were read and

I marched them down the halls toward our home room. My students entered the homeroom and took seats. They all looked at me expecting to hear some dynamic words of wisdom. I looked back at them and said to myself, "What do I do next?" I had never even talked to a group before. I said to myself, "I know what I'll do. I'll make it up as I go along." So, I started by introducing myself and said how excited I was to be their new homeroom teacher. I then had them introduce themselves. It all seemed to be going pretty well. Then a student in the back raised his hand and said his friend next to him wanted to be known as "the Jolly Green Giant." I had the young man stand up. He was six feet, seven inches tall and in the eighth grade. He had been in the eighth grade for a long time.

My job, I was told, was to prepare these students to take the city-wide exam at the end of the year in preparation for their first year in high school. As I soon found out, many couldn't even read at a first-grade level. But not being a quitter, I said to myself, "We'll just have to do the best we can with the tools the Good Lord gave us to work with." And so my year began. I decided early that year to forget about teaching grammar and spelling. Instead, I used books, novels, stories, and poetry to teach Basic English skills. And you know what—it worked! My students, by the end of that first year, thought I was a great teacher. I must have really fooled them. As a way of saying thanks, they pooled their money and bought me a 35mm camera as a gift to show their appreciation. What they didn't know was that I learned as much from them as they had learned from me. What a year!

I spent two years teaching English and Social Studies to these seventh and eighth graders, who seemed to have many other things on their mind than simply education.

In 1966, I needed additional money for my growing family. I left teaching and entered the world of business as a management trainee with a division of General Motors. After spending two years as a front-line supervisor, I left this General Motors division and accepted a position with Occidental Chemical Company, located in Niagara Falls, New York, in the capacity of training supervisors. My job was to train supervisors and to initiate and write a monthly plant newsletter, which would be sent to all employees of this two-thousand-person facility. It would delve into all the monthly happenings at the plant.

To my surprise, I became a very good trainer and writer. And over the next five years, I was promoted to substantially more and more responsible positions.

In 1969, the US government was trying to design a system to identify all of its citizens (naturally, this was way before the Internet and computers). It was felt that either through numbers or letters, the United States would have a citizen-identification system. Yes, there were social security numbers, but Congress wasn't sure this was the best identifier. To solve this issue, Congress contacted a number of companies and asked for their input. They did this by setting up a subcommittee staffed by business managers from a variety of companies.

Hooker Chemical/Occidental Chemical was contacted at its headquarters in Niagara Falls and was requested to submit a candidate for the committee who would spend some time in Washington discussing this issue and making a recommendation to Congress. I was selected.

If my memory serves me right, the committees met three or four times looking at all the possibilities. Our final recommendation was that the social security number system was already being used and it didn't make sense to set up a whole new numbering or lettering system. The cost would be outrageous. The recommendation was accepted, and to this day the social security number is the primary means of identification.

In the early 1970s, Occidental Chemical was accused of burying hazardous chemical residue in a small ditch, which they called "Love Canal." Perhaps you have heard the story, which seemed to drag on for about ten years and really initiated the whole environmental movement that we know today. In point of fact (and I was there), the chemical waste was buried in this canal, but let me tell you the rest of the story because what you heard and read about was mostly inaccurate.

In the early years of the twentieth century, there were numerous chemical companies within the United States developing and providing numerous types of chemicals to end-product manufacturers such as automobile, clothing, food, medical supplies, hospitals, etc. Within all these industries, chemicals became a vital ingredient to the design and manufacture of the commodities they produced. DuPont, Diamond Shamrock, Occidental, GE, etc., became large companies because they supplied these end-product manufacturers with necessary chemicals without which they couldn't have produced their products. However, we should realize that when chemicals are manufactured, there is and must be some waste product that must be disposed of in some way. This hasn't changed to this day. The standard practice and laws in the early part of the twentieth century was to bury the waste and to cover it with a clay cap. This, it was felt, would contain the waste products as long as the general public knew what was buried there. It was legal and considered environmentally standard practice.

Occidental Chemical (or, as it was formerly known, Hooker Chemical) followed the same legal procedures at the time. However, the city of Niagara Falls was looking for open space to build a community park. Occidental officials met with city officials and a plan was developed. The Love Canal property would deed over to the city to build a much-needed, open-space park. This would have been an ideal situation had the city actually followed the guidelines.

Occidental, via memorandum and letter, agreed to the deeding on the condition that the property is developed into this park and have no other use. Well, things didn't work out that way. The city decided that it needed more property tax dollars and made an about-face. Instead of the park, city officials decided to sell the land to potential additional residents. Hooker/Occidental, on numerous occasions, went to city officials and told them this was a dangerous, foolhardy idea and they documented their concerns in writing as well. I saw the memos. Did the city follow this advice? No! Instead, they allowed people to build, to buy lots, to dig basements, to build homes, and let residents move in.

Well, some years later, residents began to experience these waste chemicals leaking into their basements and this was, therefore, the beginning of the Love Canal debacle. We all know where this led, but what I just told you didn't really get publicized at the time and the rest of the country hopped on the bandwagon against a great big corporate polluter. It was finally resolved some twenty years later, with Occidental agreeing to pay an enormous fine.

But there is more to this story. It seems strange that during this whole process Occidental decided to move its chemical companies corporate office to Houston. Many senior executives were therefore moved to Texas. During this period Oxy also terminated the former president and hired a new man away from another chemical company, who would now be based in Houston.

Unfortunately this didn't end the environmental debacle (I'm sure Occidental hoped it would). Shortly after assessing his new role as president of Occidental Chemical Company, he was approached by the national news media. Up to this point the news media didn't seem to be a major problem to U.S. corporations. And it wouldn't have been a major problem with occidental either, except the new president, although having an outstanding chemical background, had zero public relation skills. He was totally unprepared for what was about to happen. I believe it was in 1977 that Occidental Chemical was approached by the national news media to provide full clarification of this "love canal" event. The battle lines were drawn. A major TV prime time interview show was scheduled with Mike Wallace as the inquisitor. For Occidental, it was a disaster. If the country wasn't convinced about guilt prior to this show- it certainly was now. And, as you know, this litigation went on for years with Occidental finally paying enormous penalties and fines.

In 1976, as the Love Canal' issue was boiling and becoming a major national catastrophe, I was offered a chance to work at Occidental's new corporate headquarters, located in Houston, Texas. The company wanted me to help install a computerized personnel data system to better control and track all human resources within the chemical company. To me, it was a brand-new challenge and a brand-new world. Not many companies at that time had a sophisticated way to keep track of all their employees. My role was to represent all the human resource users throughout the country while computer-technical people would build this major database.

This meant moving my family from a small town in western New York to a major metropolis. This was not easy, since I had three teenagers in high school at the time. I certainly was not the most popular person in our household, but we did it and it worked.

This move, although very difficult, brought my five children a better view of the present world that we live in. I believe in the long run it was beneficial for them, for my wife, and for me as well.

4

A TURN IN THE ROAD

IN 1978, A new, small chemical company in Houston approached me and offered me a HR position. The company was a joint venture between a research facility and a large chemical manufacturer. It had three plants in Texas with a domestic manufacturing headquarters located there as well. It had six hundred employees and needed a better way to train supervisors, to establish a college recruiting program with five southwest conference schools and engineering schools, and to put in place a succession-planning system whereby they could develop their own senior management. I decided to take a gamble and accepted the company's offer.

My role was to be an internal consultant in human resources. I could help the company do all these things aimed at the future. Over the next two years, I did these things at all the company's facilities in Texas. My reputation for achievement was growing. At the time, this company had a corporate headquarters in Princeton, New Jersey. Word of my successes had reached the corporate offices, and one day I was approached by the CEO. (Chief executive officer) and the vice president of HR, who asked me to accept an HR position with the corporate office in Princeton. This meant another move for my family, but it seemed to be a great opportunity and so I accepted. The company's name was Oxirane. Its domestic manufacturing headquarters, as I mentioned, was in Houston, but it had a European headquarters located in London. My first job was to incorporate some of the programs I had initiated in Texas within the company's three plants in Europe. After several trips to London and Amsterdam and successfully installing the HR programs, a change was about to take place.

Oxirane was purchased by one of those parties in the joint venture, ARCO Chemical! Our offices in Princeton were closed and the company shifted its base to Philadelphia, Pennsylvania. Thus, my position in human resources was moved to the city of brotherly love as well.

Shortly after taking up my new spot in Philadelphia's center city, my first assignment was to help put in place a succession-planning system for ARCO Chemical's management. Since my role had always been about developing people, I was put in charge of enrolling key managerial candidates for the chemical company in a program operated by the parent company in California, Atlantic Richfield, which is a major oil conglomerate.

As a side note, have you ever wondered why you can't fill up your car with ARCO gasoline anywhere east of the Mississippi?

The story I am about to tell you took place at ARCO's training center, located in Santa Barbara, California, in the early 1980s. The center was a gorgeous facility on a cliff overlooking the Pacific Ocean. Its purpose was to develop key leaders to oversee all of ARCO's business ventures. Each division was to pick two of its upcoming stars and send them to Santa Barbara to participate with other divisions in training sessions preparing them for senior management positions.

The program was two weeks in length, conducted four times per year. Candidates were sent from all over the world to participate and get to know each other and the company in greater detail. My role was to designate the participants from the chemical division, which I did. However, several days prior to departure for my first group, one of our candidates had a family emergency and was forced to withdraw. My supervisor said I should attend in his place. I was elated! I accepted.

The corporate retreat facility was astounding. Rooms were provided. Top-notch meals were served. Travel was first-class. It was a picturesque facility set on a California cliff. The view was astonishing.

The first week was designed to get participants to know one another. On the first day, a group of approximately forty was divided into teams of about seven or eight. Each team was given a major problem to solve for the company. Instructions were provided and the teams were dismissed to begin their deliberations.

Our team was given the problem of determining a way to improve the oil company's profitability. Each team was to present its solutions on the Friday of the first week to a group of ARCO senior executives. Since my background was in human resources and training/development, I was elected facilitator for our group. I would present our problem resolution on Friday!

After several days of serious discussions, our group came up with a fact that would lead to our recommended solution.

The majority of ARCO's oil came from the north coast of Alaska and very little came from the Middle East (where most US oil came from). Since the majority of oil is drilled, collected, and shipped via tanker to the East Coast of the United States, our solution became clear. We put together a dynamic presentation for our Friday session, recommending that since most of ARCO's oil came from Alaska's North Slope, perhaps refineries and sales should be concentrated on the West Coast. The cost savings would enhance profitability in the millions of dollars.

Now, you must remember that any solution or proposals implemented naturally became the property of Atlantic Richfield. Our presentation was outstanding, enlisting a standing ovation from all in attendance.

Now, whether our proposal ever became an impetus to modify ARCO's business plan, I really can't say for sure, but about five or six years later, I read in the *Wall Street Journal* that ARCO had decided to concentrate most of its gasoline refineries, production, and sales west of the Mississippi, which follows the same pattern to this day.

It just goes to show you never know which way the road is going to turn or where it's going to take you. Shadows continue to change. Stay open to all possibilities in front of you and follow what you think is right. But that's not to say that all decisions we make have to be the right ones. In fact, it's really through our mistakes that we learn. Without mistakes, we'd never be able to grow. And my next career mistake was a doozy.

5

BACK TO THE BEGINNING

IT DIDN'T WORK. One day in early 1982, I decided to start my own human resource business. The decision was not made lightly. I researched and researched before I made the commitment, but finally decided that if I ever wanted to start my own HR consulting business, now was the time to do it. And if I didn't take the chance now, I probably never would. My family was supportive.

I was going back to the beginning and starting from scratch. I am sure, Sheila, you may have felt the same way. To run and operate a business on one's own and be one's own business is everybody's American dream and I presume it was yours as well, and could be yours in the future.

However, at the start of my turn, it was exciting and illuminating. We had business cards printed. We purchased office equipment and borrowed enough money with a home equity loan to maintain the business for its first year or until we got established. For the first month, everything was great. I was consumed with all the details of making it successful. However, I'd overlooked a major detail. While the business structure was appropriate, we had no customers. We should have made many business contacts before starting the venture and established a possible contact stream. I should have joined several HR organizations, where networking would be possible and expected. This would have developed a contact list from which to operate.

It was very difficult trying to develop a customer base from scratch. What made it even worse, it was a year when the United States was slipping into a recession and companies were cutting back on everything except necessities. And most companies at that time felt human resources were not a necessity.

The business struggled for six months. At the end of that period, I decided I needed to change strategies and obtain another human resources position with a viable company.

I was lucky in my search and found an HR management position with a small chemical company located in Portsmouth, Virginia. Its name was Virginia Chemicals. This began the next chapter of my resurrection. My shadows kept moving.

6

VIRGINIA CHEMICALS; A STRANGE TWIST IN THE WIND

OUR MOVE TO Virginia was fairly smooth. My new company was head-quartered in Portsmouth. Again, it was a small company with about six hundred employees, scattered between four plants. One was located in Portsmouth; one in Rock Hill, South Carolina; one in Mobile, Alabama; and one in Dallas, Texas. My job was to build appropriate training programs in sales, customer service, and supervision. I even had my own facility in which to build and conduct appropriate programs. The first two years went extremely well with the company. And I became a very trusted confidant whom all parties relied on for development solutions to a variety of problems.

In those years, the company acquired a very positive reputation and profitability soared. Now I was about to learn another major lesson. When a small company does very well, other companies in similar business environments take notice. In 1985, our company was purchased by the Celanese Corporation, based in New York City.

As often happens in a buyout, many jobs in the acquired company can be impacted. Employees, through no fault of their own, wound up being downsized. This happens because the acquiring company has many of the same jobs and feels that new work can be folded in with their present staff. In other words, the terminations can save the acquiring company in some cases millions in employment costs. It is simply a fact of business life.

So, I was fired! Many other employees were fired as well. It is disheartening when you feel you are doing a good job and all of the sudden the rug is pulled out from under you. Emotions run high when good employees are terminated. It happens all across the country when one company takes over another. And believe me, regardless of what a company says it's always the acquiring company that comes out ahead. Many times we hear it's a "merger of equals". Well, believe me, there is always one that is more equal than the other.

My position changed! I wasn't really fired, yet. My role was now to know to find a consulting company who could help all those employees affected. It was then I learned about what is now called the outplacement business. We contracted with a company named Payne-Lendman. They provided seminars and individual help to all employees who were "downsized". They were very helpful and I was extremely impressed. And because of my background in training and business they offered me an opportunity to join them as a career counselor. I accepted the challenge and again changed career direction.

I found this new role very exciting but found myself traveling 80% of the time throughout the U.S. to work with individuals and groups in a wide variety of businesses.

Sheila, I'd like to tell you a story which illustrates the kind of challenges I faced in this new role. And that is what chapter 7 is about.

7

The Curious Story of Alex Ritchey

Alex was a star that never rose. He was part of what we might consider baseball legend that few knew about. The following is a true story; only Alex's last name has been changed. Alex was an outstanding high school baseball player. He had real potential. He was destined for the major leagues. And he would become a star everywhere. However, there was one major obstacle in the path and that is what this story is about. I met Alex in the mid-1980s. I was working as an outplacement counselor in Virginia Beach, Virginia. As I told you, my job was to counsel and teach people how to find a new job.

If you saw the movie *Up in the Air*, you would have a good idea of what my company did. However, there was a major difference. In the movie, George Clooney's character was hired to come in and terminate the staff.

In reality, my company played a different role. We were brought in to assist those being terminated. We did not actually fire people. We would, on the other hand, teach managers how to do it with as much compassion as possible. Then we would immediately begin to work with "those caught in the crunch."

For example, let's say a GE plant in San Jose, California, had to reduce its head count by one hundred people. The company would fly me to San Jose to be available as soon as the termination began. I would be in the next room or conference center as soon as each individual was told his or her job was being eliminated. The terminated employees would then be ushered in to meet with me. My job was to help each person with the healing process and identify how to take the next logical step in his or her life. I would help them write resumes and letters, teach them interview skills, and give them practice in how to sell the product—themselves. In the few years that I did this, I worked with more than two thousand people—male and female, young and old, rich and poor. And I became very effective at it.

One of the most interesting clients, however, was a short, heavyset, older man whose position as marketing specialist had been eliminated. He had worked for a company in Newport News, Virginia. His name was Alex Ritchey. He had just been fired!

Now, sometimes I conducted a three-day group workshop with the downsized, and sometimes the sessions were what we called "one-on-ones." The "one-on-ones" were very individualized as I would work with clients until they found their next position. It was very intense, requiring close interaction between the candidate and the counselor.

Now, when people are first told their position is being eliminated, they go through a wide range of emotions. Sometimes they cry. There's anger. They're bitter. And sometimes they are even accepting and understanding of it. But it was the counselor's job to work with whatever emotion they came in with and reassure them that there was a future for them—many times an even brighter future than they had expected if they stayed where they were. I thought I had seen it all, and then I met Alex.

Alex was very quiet. He didn't want to say anything. He just sat there and let me do all the talking. This was not the way it was supposed to happen. To get clients started on the next track mandated that we learn as much as possible about each client. They're assured this is a very confidential process. We guarantee it. And all of our clients eventually welcome the help. Each one, by the end of the first day, always agreed to the help, but not Alex. No matter what I tried, I could not gain his confidence. By the end of the second day, I was almost ready to turn him over to another counselor—apparently; he didn't want to trust me. And our work together demanded it.

Finally, I told him that it might be best for him to work with someone else. We had many good counselors who did what I did, and they were all good, each in their own way. Alex stared at me for what seemed like an hour. Finally, he said, "I have nothing against you or even my former company. I just figure my career and my life are over! I'm too old and tired to find something new."

I said, "Alex, you'd be amazed at the different people I have been able to help. It comes down to having confidence in what I can do for you in working with me, but I need to know who you really are, which allows me then to build a background sketch of what you have to sell to the next company." Alex looked straight at me and thought for a long time. Finally, he said, "I'm going to tell you a story that I have never told anyone in my life. It's a story that goes back to the 1950s. I was an outstanding catcher for my baseball team in upstate New York. I was an all-star and considered the best baseball catcher in New York state—no exaggeration. In my senior year of high school, I was approached by a scout from the New York Yankees. He watched me play, talked to my parents and me about joining the Yankees upon graduation. I was excited and felt this would be my future.

"I signed a standard rookie contract, and after graduation joined the Yankee farm system. I reported to their minor league team, which was a single-A team, where usually all rookies began. From the day I put on a team uniform and began practicing, my star began to rise. The manager said I was an outstanding find. From the first day, he said I had a natural gift. I would not be playing single-A for long. He was right. Within a few weeks, I was moved up to double-A. And shortly thereafter to triple-A, which is the division a player, joins prior to being brought up to the major leagues. I finished the season in triple-A and then began the next season in triple-A, as well. Why? Well, the New York Yankees had a great catcher in Yogi Berra, who was almost invincible.

However, partway through that second season, Yogi suffered an injury—not serious, but it would keep him out of several games. The call was made and I was brought up to the Yankees. I was ecstatic! The big team, me—Alex Ritchey!

"But I was about to learn a major lesson. The first game I played was a game we were losing in the late innings. However, we managed to load the bases and I was coming to bat. My chance had finally come and I was going to make the most of it. The third-base coach gave me the bunt sign. The pitch came in perfect and it was sweet. I had an instant to make a decision. I towered it over the right-field fence, bringing in four runs and the fans went crazy. It was bedlam. I felt ten feet tall. As I crossed the plate, Casey Stengel, who was our manager, was waiting for me. I thought he was going to hug me, but instead, in a very even voice, he said, "This is your last game, kid. Apparently you can't follow instructions. You won't be playing ball for me."

Now, back in those days there was no union representing players. Contracts were written in such a way that players had very few rights.

"I never played in another game," Alex continued. "I sat the bench for two or three years, hoping for a chance, but it never happened. They refused to trade me as well.

"After about five years, I just gave it up and decided to find a job. That incident has affected my whole life and my whole career. I could never get over it!"

Once I knew this, I was able to help him put a whole different spin on his career search. His attitude changed, and in about a month, he found a position in marketing, which was even better than the one he left—after all these years it helped him immensely to open up a closed door and get past it and develop a strategy for the future.

Job loss is a very traumatic event. It helps to have someone to confide in who can understand the feelings one is going through. Job counselors are not miracle workers but just good listeners that encourage candidates not to give up. There is a career future for everyone—rich and poor, young and old, black and white. It's a matter of continuing to work the process, not giving up no matter how difficult it seems. Success is always obtainable for everyone, whether you are eighteen or eighty.

8

ANOTHER CHANGE OF DIRECTION; AND LET'S MEET TIM McVEIGH

In 1987, a recruiting firm in western New York approached me about a move back to Buffalo to reinvigorate a corporate training operation that had lost its direction. It would be like going home for my family and me. Over the span of five months and numerous interviews with all the key executives, I was offered the position of assistant vice president for corporate training and development for a very small local financial services company in western New York. In the seven years I was with this company, I provided assistance in changing the direction of an old-time, established banking operation into a major player in providing financial services throughout the eastern United States. This is not to say that the company's success was due totally to my efforts, because that is not the case. The ball was already in motion when I joined the firm and I simply provided an additional nudge in the right direction.

It was exciting to help a company whose stock was listed at $35 a share in 1987 to achieve a pinnacle of over $500 a share in 1993. To this day, it is a well-run financial services company, which looks at itself not as a staid, old conservative bank, but as a dynamic future-oriented business that has all the pieces in the right place.

But, as in most companies politics plays a bigger role than people believe. Let me tell you another story which you might call a real adventure.

I had been working for this bank about seven years and had just been promoted the previous year from Assistant VP to Vice President. I had designed and installed a succession planning system for which I received a $30,000 bonus. The bank was doing well and so was I, at least I thought I was.

Then one day my firm absorbed the remnants of a local failed saving and loan company. My boss inherited a females human resources Vice President. As a result he redesigned his HR organization placing her in charge of training and development and the employment administrative services function. From that first day, she and I never really got along.

After about six months it was rumored she was having an affair with my former boss's boss. Whether she was or not is pure conjecture.

All I do know is that one day my former boss set up a time to meet with me. After my previous very good year, I thought I was being promoted. I was excited!

"We're going to have to let you go. We've decided to go in a different direction. We'll continue your pay and benefits for three months and provide out-placement assistance". This was his statement to me on that historic day!

I was devastated. I couldn't believe it! I was flabbergasted. It was like a punch in the face from the blind side. But you say to yourself, what can I do about it? You play it over and over again in your mind and you finally come to the conclusion- nothing! You have to pick up your tool box and move on. Life is a learning experience. You can be depressed. You can be down trodden. You can crawl into bed and pull the covers over your head. You can be like the ostrich and bury your head in the sand. And it is easy to fall into this abyss.

But, Sheila, like the title of this book "Life is what you make it", you can't give up. To survive you must look at is as an educational experience and each person really has the ability to do exactly that.

It was exciting to me to play a part in the growth of this company. By 1993, my job was completed. I had helped the firm change operations significantly and it was time for me to move on.

From 1993 to 1996, I worked as an HR consultant for a company by the name of Resultants International, helping provide training and HR operational assistance for several companies along the eastern seaboard. But the company's business model was changing as well and it was time for me to move on again. The shadows had shifted again.

In 1996, I was hired as an internal human resources consultant to help a Delaware-based Uniform Services Company reenergize itself. However, I didn't move directly to Delaware; instead, the company's controller offered to let me stay with him at his home in an effort to help me cut expenses.

My role here was to help settle several internal human resources issues. It was a small company headquartered in Wilmington, Delaware, with facilities in Lancaster, Pennsylvania, Washington, DC, and New Jersey. The company's business was to retrieve, clean, and restore uniforms. The clients: hospitals, doctors' offices, service stations, and other facilities that utilized uniforms. My role was to put in place appropriate training programs to ensure regulatory compliance within this sales and service industry. The company also wanted an appropriate management development program that could be available to all associates.

One day after work, I returned to the home in which I was residing and saw a sketch on television of a person being sought for the bombing of a federal building in Oklahoma City. I said to my friend, John, "Wow! That person in the sketch looks just like my cousin, Tim McVeigh, but that's impossible. He lives in my old hometown of Lockport, New York, as a well-liked young man. He only recently had been discharged honorably from the military."

Well, I was soon to find that my young cousin was indeed the person that the federal authorities were searching for. He was considered the first American terrorist and, yet, the person I knew was a well-liked young man who had his whole life before him. I remember him at our family Christmas parties and at picnics in western New York as a solid member of our family. For some reason, he had developed a strong hatred of the US government. He felt the government was trying to take away most of the freedoms that the constitution had provided for its citizens. To this day, I don't understand how he developed this extreme attitude. I know he applied to join the US Special Forces before leaving the military and I know for some reason he was turned down.

Over the next several months, as investigation into his suspected involvement in the bombing continued, each person in my family was investigated and questioned, and it didn't matter where in the United States we lived. The FBI got to us all. My meeting was held at the FBI office in Wilmington. As I told them, I was astonished and astounded by those allegations. I remembered him as a well-liked young man who was preparing for his life as a civilian. I found it unbelievable.

Every year, our family, on the McVeigh side, had an annual Christmas Eve party attended by all family members. That year, I remember the party was held at my Cousin Bill McVeigh's house. During the evening, Bill had a chance to talk with Tim by phone and offered each family member a chance to talk with Tim as well. When my turn came, I expressed my utter shock to Tim and said that I couldn't believe he really carried out the bombing. I offered to write a story from his perspective. His statement to me was, "No, cousin Don! I don't want anyone else to get involved." And that was the last time I talked with him.

My cousin Bill still lives in his small home in Lockport, New York. Diane Sawyer of ABC News spent much time with Bill in trying to analyze "why" I believe they still stay as friends. Tim's two sisters have moved on with their lives. And his mother died several years later.

It was the end of a tragic tale. I will never forget because I don't think I ever heard the whole story and the shadow never stands still for long.

While with the uniform company, Sheila, I did complete my master's degree in business. And at the conclusion of my tenure with the company, I moved back to western New York, which is what my wife wanted me to do all along. But the saga doesn't quite end there.

9

THE WORLD IS WHAT YOU MAKE OF IT!

AFTER I RETURNED to western New York, Sheila, a friend of mine suggested I call the Business Department at Villa Maria College as the department was looking to hire someone to teach an accounting course on a part-time basis. That's how I started teaching here at Villa. For several semesters, I taught only accounting. I also did career counseling for another outplacement firm in Buffalo.

In 1999, the Business Department's head was going to retire. And since I had been a pretty good college instructor, she asked if I wanted to take over her position as department head. I agreed and accepted, and that's why you find me here today. I hope I haven't bored you with this long tale, but there are even more pieces that I could have added, for example: working for the American Red Cross, working in sales, selling cars, modeling, and making commercials.

I think the main concept I want to emphasize, Sheila, is that, yes, shadows keep shifting, moving, and life is a journey. We choose how we want to take that journey and we can be winners or losers.

We're all familiar with this statement: "For every action there is an equal reaction." It's found in most high school physics books. This phrase, in its usual context, relates to the world of physical science. But it can be applied equally well to the world of human behavior. For every action that we consciously take in life there will be a negative and a positive reaction. It is this series of reactions beginning in childhood that determines our future patterns of behavior as we grow and accumulate both positive and negative attitudes toward the actions we take or others take. These attitudes reinforce a particular behavior pattern that we follow throughout our lives. The basketball player who drives himself to become the best and consequently moves into professional ranks does so because past experience has shown that this has to be good and to be a course that he should pursue. The individual who overcomes seemingly insurmountable odds to achieve a lifelong goal does so because of something or someone in his or her past. The reaction to what was said or done becomes the driving force toward the ultimate achievement of the goal, as it was in my case. No one is born to win, Sheila. People learn how to win by looking at their winning or losing experiences, analyzing them and modifying behavior and/or methods into vehicles for winning.

You don't win by losing, but you can win something in losing. Although this sounds like a contradiction, it's not. We're all subject to usual human feeling and, therefore, we can't be 100 percent successful at everything we do. If an individual is broad-minded enough to look upon a loss as an educational experience and can say, "Hey, I lost, but why did I lose?" and recognize the reason for the loss, that person will have gained something, the knowledge of what it takes to win.

What I'm suggesting is that you turn a negative into a positive. In spite of failure, you must think, act, and believe that this failure is not irredeemable. If you can maintain a positive attitude in spite of a negative outcome, the lessons learned from a series of setbacks can be turned into a positive force for the future.

This might sound easy, but in most cases it's not. Too often, a great many negatives tend to undermine a positive outlook. It takes a great effort sometimes to overcome this attitude. But you should keep in mind that anyone can train himself or herself to do this, and if the individual is successful, those things in life that he or she desires will be within grasp.

It's imperative that you face a loss head-on. Don't back away. Be aggressive and confident and you can succeed.

Let me give you a case in point, Sheila. A man I knew once, Fred Bishop, was a winner. Fred began as a management trainee in a major technology-based corporation. He was a recent graduate with a degree in business administration and he was considered excellent managerial material by his supervisors. After his training period was over, Fred immediately moved into a managerial position in the firm's highly prestigious and highly competitive marketing division. Fred had done an excellent job during his training period, and his supervisors recommended him and approved his request to start his career in marketing. He had shown initiative and enthusiasm in the job, often working overtime to do certain extra assignments, and had demonstrated his talents and abilities. Fred continued to show these traits in his first few months as a manager, but after a year, he shifted into low gear, as many of us often do. He began coming in a few minutes late every now and then and very rarely worked overtime. Fred's work was still excellent. His supervisor began to think that Fred wasn't cut out to be a top management candidate.

One day, Fred was surprised to learn that a coworker of his, who had started her management training with Fred, had just been promoted to a top management position in the division. Fred, who had his eyes on that job for some time, mulled over the situation and analyzed the reasons for his coworker's success, Fred realized that she had always shown enthusiasm for the work and had taken initiative in coming up with new ideas and suggestions to improve the division's marketing activities. He knew that she often stayed a half an hour or more late, and did one or two additional projects or reports than was necessary. Fred knew that her actions had not escaped the eyes of their supervisors or his. Fred shook his head, wondering how he could have let himself slip. He was determined to change his attitude. He worked. The following year, when another top management position opened up in the marketing division, Fred was considered above all others in the department and got the job.

The ability to succeed at what you do is not an inherited trait. Of course, we do hear of those people who are born with a "silver spoon in their mouth." But even those people don't become winners until they are able to take the right steps toward whatever goal they're aiming for.

Some can do it. Some can't. Winning doesn't come naturally for every-one. It takes great effort, and the ability to learn from one's successes and failures. If you can do this, then you too can succeed at whatever you do.

As I said before, Sheila, if you can use this life saga in any way, please do. I'd be interested in reading your English assignment when it's completed. You never know. I just might be able to learn something from it as my own journey continues! Remember, the end is also the beginning. Shadows keep moving until the day is done, but as the sun shines the shadows will return. And if we learn from what the previous day taught us, we'll have taken one more step toward the horizon. Experience is a funny thing, Sheila. When you're very young, you feel you already know it all. Why should I go to college? In school, why take subjects I'll never use? It seems to be a waste of time. I've got more important things to do. But the older you become, you begin to see that you know less and less about more and more. And, Sheila, if you have learned anything from this discussion at all, it's that stories can help educate and that is what I attempt to do in each of my courses. Provide each student a chance to learn from my adventures. All you have to do is become an active listener, which you have been. Thanks for your time, Sheila.

- THE END -

LIFE IS WHAT YOU MAKE IT

TODAY ONE OF my grandchildren died of a drug overdose! He was thirty-four. It did not come as a surprise. As I said before, Sheila, life is what you make it, and since the time he was sixteen years old, he began making the life that got him. His parents tried, but...

As Bill O'Reilly stated in his book *Keep It Pithy*, "Again, it all comes back to the free will that I believe we all have. Even though a child has it rough, there will come a time when he or she, like all human beings, is faced with a clear choice. Either become a productive citizen or become a problem."

For some, the choices come early, perhaps even in the sixth or seventh grade. For others, the choice comes later. Parents can be a guiding force here, but the individual has to make the choice. And his or her peer group can be a big factor in this choice. When the individual begins to trust the peer group rather than the parent, the train can begin to leave the track.

Life is not necessarily easy. Many times, kids have to make these critical choices before they're ready to make these choices. To me, it seems very important that we, as parents, provide a solid education from the time our children are born, and that includes the three Rs—responsibility, respect, religion—until they become teenagers.

"Sheila, my wife and I have five children and when they were about to begin their teen years, it was a major concern for me. Did we do enough that would enable them to make those right decisions? In a way, we were lucky because the temptations in the '60s and '70s were much different than today."

As one pastor said, "Life is like a monopoly game. We play the game accumulating 'things'—cars, houses, properties, money. Like the little girl in the GEICO commercial says, 'We want more, more, more.' And the objective in the monopoly game is to accumulate the most. If you win the game you are very excited. You've defeated all the other players! But the interesting thing is...the elation and excitement only lasts a short time. Then you have to put everything back in the box and the game is over!

And that is life! You can't take all these worldly possessions with you when you die. Let's face it, we all will die and I've never seen a hearse towing a U-Haul.

"Sheila, it's how you live life that matters. Did you do the best you could with all the gifts the good lord has 'loaned' you? Because, we have to leave all those gifts behind. The only things that survive are the good works we've left behind."

A shadow is a funny thing when you think about it, Sheila. It's here today and gone tomorrow. And that is life!!!